Sharon Aseerwatham

mary-kate olsen   **ashley** olsen

ourstory

mary-kate olsen   ashley olsen

ourstory

Mary-Kate and Ashley Olsen's
Official Biography

As told to Damon Romine

HarperEntertainment
An Imprint of HarperCollinsPublishers

A PARACHUTE PRESS BOOK

A PARACHUTE PRESS BOOK

Parachute Publishing, L.L.C.
156 Fifth Avenue
Suite 302
New York, NY 10010

Published by
≝HarperEntertainment
An Imprint of HarperCollins*Publishers*
10 East 53rd Street, New York, NY 10022-5299

Created and produced by
Parachute Publishing, L.L.C., in cooperation with Dualstar Publications,
a division of Dualstar Entertainment Group, LLC,
published by HarperEntertainment, an imprint of
HarperCollins Publishers.

For information address HarperCollins Publishers Inc.,
10 East 53rd Street, New York, NY 10022-5299.

ISBN 0-06-056848-8

HarperCollins®, ≝®, and HarperEntertainment™ are trademarks of
HarperCollins Publishers Inc.

First printing: September 2003

Printed in the United States of America
Visit HarperEntertainment on the World Wide Web at
www.harpercollins.com

Chapter 1

The Real Mary-Kate and Ashley

You and your friends are watching the MTV Video Music Awards on television, talking about the newest music and admiring the cool outfits the celebrities are wearing.

Then you spot your favorite stars stepping out of a limo at the end of a red carpet. You grew up watching them on television and in movies. You hold your breath as they wave to the crowd and smile into the camera.

It's Mary-Kate and Ashley Olsen. They have the life of big stars, you think. They're always so glamorous, always going to the hottest parties in Hollywood, right? Their lives seem so different from yours. But if you told that to Mary-Kate and

Ashley, they would most definitely disagree! "Most of the time we do what every other teen does," Mary-Kate says.

"Right," Ashley agrees. "We go to school, hang with our friends, and go out on dates. You know, everyday stuff."

They take shopping trips to the local boutiques, rush out to catch the latest movies, and go to the beach. They're into kickboxing, yoga, and Pilates.

"When we were younger we liked to kick around a soccer ball and we were cheerleaders. But now we're into going to the gym," Ashley says.

The sisters have crushes on celebrities and guys at school just like you do. They listen to the music of Dave Matthews, U2, and John Mayer, and go to concerts with their friends.

It may be hard to believe but Mary-Kate and Ashley lead very normal lives. They were born on June 13, 1986. (Ashley is the older twin by two minutes!) They've grown up in suburban Los Angeles with their brother, Trent, who is two years older than they are, and their little sister, Elizabeth, who is three years younger. Their parents are divorced, and Mary-Kate and Ashley divide their time between their dad and their mom. Their dad, Dave, is a mortgage broker. Their mom, Jarnette

The Real Mary-Kate and Ashley

(Jarnie), used to dance with the Los Angeles Ballet.

"Trent is a typical big brother," Mary-Kate says. "He thinks of us as his little sisters. He's very protective, but he also likes to tease us. He's great at drawing and sports. He's also into volleyball."

"We miss having him around all the time, now that he's in college," Ashley adds. "But luckily he's not that far away, and he tries to come home and have dinner as often as possible."

Lizzie, their younger sister, is very independent and well rounded. She loves ballet and acting. She has made a few guest appearances in some of Mary-Kate and Ashley's videos. Right now she's not interested in becoming a professional actress, but she enjoys performing in community theater.

Mary-Kate and Ashley also have a sister and brother from their dad's second marriage to McKenzie Olsen. Taylor is six years old, and Jake is five. "It's great having little kids to play with," Ashley says. "We help out with baby-sitting a lot. With so many kids around, the house gets really crazy sometimes. But we love it!"

"Our family is a lot like everyone else's," says Mary-Kate. "Sometimes we argue. You know how it goes: One minute everyone is watching TV. The next, an argument breaks out over the remote control. But most of the time we get along great. We're very close, and we look out for one another. We all share our stuff. But the rule is you have to ask before borrowing something!"

"Mary-Kate could be a bit sneaky about 'borrowing' when she was little," reveals her mom, Jarnie. "Once, when the twins were very young, money was missing from all the kids' piggy banks."

"And suddenly Mary-Kate was very wealthy," adds their dad, Dave. "We divided the money back up and returned it to the correct piggy banks. Then Mary-Kate was benched for a while."

The Olsen household has always been filled with pets. They have had dogs, cats, birds, turtles, and hamsters. Mary-Kate recently adopted a new puppy, a black Chihuahua-poodle mix that she named Jack—plus she and Ashley have two other dogs at their dad's house. Mary-Kate also has two horses, CD and Star. She stables them at a nearby ranch.

Horseback riding is one of Mary-Kate's favorite activities. "I love it. I'd go for a riding lesson every day if I could," she says. Mary-Kate has even competed in horse shows—and has the ribbons and trophies to prove it!

While Mary-Kate is riding, Ashley keeps busy

with dance class, tennis, and, most recently, golf. Her love of dance is something she inherited from her mother. Together the girls go to yoga class, which is great mental and physical exercise.

Both girls have very close friends whom they see all the time. They each have their own special friends, of course, but they also have good friends in common. When they were younger, Mary-Kate and Ashley and their friends would go Rollerblading, to Disneyland, or to a nearby amusement park called Knott's Berry Farm. "I remember how happy I was when we were finally tall enough to get on all the rides," says Ashley. "We'd ride every roller coaster there was!"

Once the girls took some of their friends to an amusement park to film a roller coaster scene for their video, *You're Invited to Mary-Kate & Ashley's Birthday Party*. To get the scene, the whole group had to ride the roller coaster eight times in a row! "We all got so dizzy we could hardly stand," Ashley remembers.

Now that they're older, Mary-Kate and Ashley don't ride roller coasters much. They're too busy riding in their cars! Each received a brand-new car for her sixteenth birthday.

"It's great to have more freedom. Sometimes

we'll meet our friends at the beach or at the movies. Other times we just hang out at their houses," Mary-Kate says. "And when we're not driving someplace, there's always something fun to do at home—especially swimming. We have a pool in the backyard."

Ashley and Mary-Kate don't share a room. They have separate rooms at both their mom's and their dad's places. At their dad's, the rooms are down the hall from each other. They love the shabby-chic style of design, and their rooms are decorated with pretty fabric patterns and tons of fluffy pillows.

Both girls have lots of pictures on the walls—pictures of friends, cast photos from movies they've worked on, and places they've visited all over the world. They also display photos of their parents and brothers and sisters.

Mary-Kate and Ashley each have their own stereo and TV in their bedrooms. When asked about their favorite TV shows, they answer at the exact same time: "We like *Will & Grace* and *Friends*!" They might add "late-night infomercials" to that list, too—both girls admit to falling asleep with the TV on!

When Mary-Kate and Ashley became teens, they got their own computers. They were so excited, they took a typing course in school so they could type really fast on the keyboard. Both are hooked on the Internet, and they research subjects on the World Wide Web for school. And, of course, their friends across the country and around the world are just a click away through e-mail. Mary-Kate, especially, likes to keep in touch with all the friends she makes when they film a movie far from home.

The sisters—and their parents—take school very seriously. Their parents make sure that Mary-Kate and Ashley are getting the best education possible. Even when Mary-Kate and Ashley are working on a TV show or a movie, they don't miss a day of class. The classroom just has to go where they go!

"A lot of people probably think that going on location must be cool because then we get to miss school," says Ashley. "Wrong!"

"The law says we have to spend at least three hours each day in school and do a ton of homework while we're working," Mary-Kate explains. "Besides, when we're done shooting and go back home, we don't want to be behind the rest of our class."

Mary-Kate and Ashley keep up with their classmates by having studio teachers right there on the set. The studio teachers give all the same homework and tests that their regular teachers give. Usually they have one teacher for language arts,

French, and social studies and one for math and science.

The girls do well in all their school subjects. In fact, they like to compete with each other for the highest grades. "Ashley makes me work harder," Mary-Kate says. "If I don't do as well as Ashley on a test, I'll go over the subject again."

"The same goes for me," Ashley adds.

Ashley's favorite subject is math. Mary-Kate enjoys English and creative writing. Sometimes Mary-Kate will write short stories on her own. And sometimes they both keep journals when they visit new places.

Ashley and Mary-Kate say their studio teachers can be tough when necessary to make sure all their homework gets done. "Sometimes they'll crack the whip to make sure we finish on time," Mary-Kate admits. "But actually, *we* want to get it done and over with just as much as they do!"

When the sisters are doing a TV show, the studio classroom looks just like a regular classroom—with desks, computers, and maps on the walls. But when Mary-Kate and Ashley are traveling to make a movie, they use any room that is available. "We've had classrooms in trailers, in lobbies—once even in a large closet!" Ashley remembers.

The Real Mary-Kate and Ashley

At the time this book was printed, Mary-Kate and Ashley were hard at work studying for finals and for their college entrance exams. "It's tough work," Mary-Kate says, "but we know we have to do it if we want to get into a good college."

But it's not all about work for Mary-Kate and Ashley. They try to have as much fun as possible while they're on the set. That's not always easy, though. Sometimes people are a little nervous being around them at first. But it doesn't take long for people to realize that Mary-Kate and Ashley don't *act* famous.

"I met Mary-Kate and Ashley on the set of *Holiday in the Sun*," recalls Billy Brown, an actor and friend who has appeared in three of their movies and on the television show *So Little Time*. "It was my first big break and I was excited to meet them. I was surprised at how shy they were at first. But then we got to talking, and they're really nice and a lot of fun. I have a blast every time I work with them."

They do their best to make everyone feel really comfortable. And Mary-Kate and Ashley are the first to reach out and help others in need. "They're genuinely good, sweet, compassionate girls," their studio teacher says.

Mary-Kate and Ashley: Our Story

So how can Mary-Kate and Ashley be stars *and* be so much like you and your friends? They say they have their mom and dad to thank.

"The most important thing our parents have taught us is to respect other people," Mary-Kate says. "After all, we're only two of six kids in our family. There's no time for special treatment."

"Yeah," Ashley agrees. "We have to clean our rooms just like everybody else."

Chapter 2

The Twin Thing

In a lot of ways Mary-Kate and Ashley are like you and your friends. And if you have a twin, then they *really* are like you!

"People ask us all the time if it's fun to be a twin," Mary-Kate says, "and we always tell them the same thing. Yes!"

"We always have each other to talk with," Ashley explains. "We share all our big secrets."

Sisters are often very close. But twin sisters are built-in best friends! Like most twins, Mary-Kate and Ashley share a special bond. Each of them often seems to know what the other is thinking—without saying a word.

"Ashley can tell things about me, like if something is bothering me—or if I think a guy is cute!" Mary-Kate says.

"We can tell what the other is feeling, but we can't read each other's mind or anything," Ashley adds. "It's more like understanding body language."

The girls have a great time together. Mary-Kate is known to be more of a prankster, but both girls have a great sense of humor. In fact, Ashley usually jumps right in on Mary-Kate's practical jokes. But it's all in the name of fun. When they're on a set, Mary-Kate and Ashley's favorite prank is to clip a clothespin on the back of a coworker's shirt. Then they'll wait—and giggle—to see how long it takes before he or she notices! "It's a long-running joke," Ashley explains. "We've been doing it since we were kids. So we keep doing it just to crack each other up."

Being a twin isn't just fun. There are other benefits, too. Think about how practical it would be to have someone who looks like you—especially if you both had the same taste in clothes.

When Mary-Kate and Ashley were younger they didn't always have to try on their clothes before buying them. Who needs a mirror when you can see how an outfit looks on your twin, right?

Unfortunately that trick doesn't work for Ashley

and Mary-Kate anymore. They still have similar taste in clothes, but Mary-Kate leans toward more funky outfits and lots of accessories, where Ashley likes classic and tailored items—and shoes, shoes, shoes!

Another example of how having a twin can come in handy was when the girls filmed their first TV movie *To Grandmother's House We Go.* Just a week before filming began, Mary-Kate scratched her eye while playing. It was red for weeks! They filmed around it as much as possible, but when it came to an important dinner scene between the two girls, Ashley got dressed like Mary-Kate and played her part too!

Of course, everyone always expects twins to trade places with each other. You've seen it on TV shows, where twins switch places to take a test in school. Or to go out on a date. Or to fool a friend. In one episode of Mary-Kate and Ashley's TV series, *TWO of a kind*, the girls switched places to fool their dad. They did it again in their TV movie *Switching Goals* and in their feature film, *It Takes Two*. But Mary-Kate and Ashley swear they've never done that in real life.

"We haven't tried it," Ashley tells us. "Our friends and family can tell us apart. So we never bothered."

Mary-Kate and Ashley were born on June 13, under the sign of Gemini. It makes sense—Gemini is the sign of twins! Geminis often have great communication skills, just like Mary-Kate and Ashley. They are fun-loving, outgoing, and quick-minded. Geminis can also adapt easily to new situations. And best of all, just like Mary-Kate and Ashley, Geminis love people—especially their friends!

Or maybe they just don't remember. "They did try some switcheroos around age five," their mom says. "But ultimately they can't fool me or their dad."

Well, most of the time, anyway. Once, when the twins were shooting a video, their dad called out, "Ashley, come here. I want to ask you something." But he was really talking to Mary-Kate! The whole film crew laughed. Their dad's mistake probably made the crew feel better about all the times *they'd* gotten Mary-Kate and Ashley mixed up.

Still, it isn't always easy to guess who's who. Everyone seems to come up with a different way to tell Mary-Kate and Ashley apart.

"Bob Saget, our TV dad on *Full House*, used to mix us up all the time when we were little," recalls Mary-Kate.

The Twin Thing

"We'd put our hands on our hips and give him our best 'Don't-you-know-me-by-now?' look," Ashley adds, laughing. "After we got a little older and he got to know our personalities, he was finally able to tell us apart."

Even their hairstylist sometimes got them confused. "He'd forget whose hair he was working on and ask, 'Which one are you again?'" Mary-Kate remembers.

But Mary-Kate and Ashley don't get mad when people mistake them for each other. They're used to it. They just smile and say, "My name is Ashley (or Mary-Kate), not Mary-Kate (or Ashley)!"

Even though the girls look so much alike, they are not identical twins. Mary-Kate and Ashley are fraternal twins. Fraternal twins sometimes look similar to each other, but they are not exactly the same.

There *are* ways to tell Mary-Kate and Ashley apart. When Mary-Kate and Ashley were infants, their parents used their freckles to figure out who was who. Now, at sixteen, Ashley is slightly taller. Mary-Kate's face is a bit rounder. Ashley is right-handed, while Mary-Kate is left-handed.

"I think we looked more alike when we were younger, but not now," Ashley says.

DID YOU KNOW?

• Spring is the time of the year that most twins are born (just like Mary-Kate and Ashley, who were born in June).

• More than half of all twins are male.

• More twins are left-handed, like Mary-Kate, than are people who are not twins.

• Fraternal twins, like Mary-Kate and Ashley, are more likely to run in the family than are identical twins.

• Female fraternal twins and their sisters are more likely to give birth to twins.

"I'm the cute one," jokes Mary-Kate. "Just kidding. Seriously, I don't think we look anything alike."

For work, the girls have often had to look as similar as possible—especially during their time on *Full House*, when they played the same part. But Ashley and Mary-Kate enjoy trying out different looks.

A couple of years ago, the sisters decided to change their hairstyle. Mary-Kate cut her hair shorter. It was cute and it looked great on her. For a while, she clearly had her own look.

There was just one problem: Ashley loved her sister's short hair—and she wanted her own hair cut the same way. Before they knew it, the girls looked alike again. Over the past few years they've tried many styles—short, long, straight, curly. Hey, they're teens and they like to experiment!

Currently the makeup look of choice for both girls is a fresh face with a hint of lip gloss for everyday. But they'll break out the makeup brushes if they have a special event to attend.

And since they have similar fashion sense, sometimes they buy the same outfits or accessories for an event, but each girl picks a different color so they never end up dressing alike.

But what happens when they both want to wear the exact same thing on the same day?

"When Mary-Kate and Ashley want to wear the same outfit, it gets a little crazy," their dad says with a laugh. He remembers when the girls were getting dressed for a concert. They both wanted to wear the same brown jacket with their black pants. This time, Mary-Kate won—and she got to wear it. (Ashley wore a blue jacket.) The next time, Ashley got to pick first. When they were younger, the girls were also known to argue over who had the cooler, more grown-up shoes.

So, how do Mary-Kate and Ashley work out their occasional differences? "We talk it over, and then we usually decide to take turns," Ashley explains. "Mary-Kate will wear something one time and I'll wear it the next time."

In fact, the girls don't compete with each other at all. Well, except for grades. "But it's good-natured, and it pushes us to do better, " Mary-Kate says.

Mary-Kate and Ashley look out for each other and give each other advice. And when they're acting, they always help each other out. For instance, during the filming of their movie *Passport to Paris*, Mary-Kate had to give a speech about Notre Dame Cathedral. It included lots of hard-to-remember words like "flying buttresses" (an architectural term)—and Mary-Kate kept tripping up on the words! Ashley gently touched her shoulder and said, "Don't worry, you'll get it." Later, when Ashley had to say a long speech in French, Mary-Kate was able to encourage *her*.

The girls make a terrific team because they are so supportive of each other. Sure, they can get on each other's nerves. All sisters do. They have sibling squabbles just like in any family. But in the end, Ashley and Mary-Kate are best friends.

"Having a twin keeps us grounded," Ashley says. "We encourage each other all the time, but we also know when to say, 'Hey, get over yourself.'"

The Twin Thing

Recently a TV interviewer asked Ashley and Mary-Kate if they wanted to go to different colleges. Mary-Kate said, "I don't think so. Going to college is such an important time in your life. You know, a new place, new people, new experiences. I don't think I could be without my sister, too."

"Me neither," Ashley agrees. "Mary-Kate has always been there for me. She's everything to me."

Chapter 3

The *Full House* Years

How did Mary-Kate and Ashley get started in show business?

It all began when they were just seven months old. Their mom took them to a modeling agency. Mary-Kate and Ashley were beautiful babies. And the fact that they were twins was a bonus. When kids are working on a movie or a television series, the law says they can work only for a few hours each day. Hiring twins means you are able to split the work between them.

The modeling agency quickly signed up both girls and lined up auditions. But Jarnie didn't expect that they would actually get work. "I just thought it might be fun," she admits. "It was a way to get out of the house and do something a little out of the ordinary."

Then Jarnie took the girls to a TV audition with executive producer Bob Boyett. Mr. Boyett was looking for young twins to play baby Michelle on a new ABC comedy. The show was called *Full House*.

By the time Mary-Kate and Ashley had their audition, there was already another set of twins in place to play the part of baby Michelle. But Mr. Boyett changed his mind when he met the Olsens. "I just thought they were so unique," he says. "They had these big expressive eyes. They were friendly, they listened when you spoke to them, and they would really respond to you!"

Plus, the girls looked a lot like the two big sisters on the TV show. Candace Cameron had been hired to play D.J., and Jodie Sweetin would play middle sister Stephanie.

Mary-Kate and Ashley were perfect for *Full House!* The fact that they were fraternal—not identical—twins could have been a problem, though. As babies, the girls looked almost exactly alike, so they could both be Michelle. But what would happen as the girls grew up? Would they still look alike?

Maybe you've seen the classic TV show *Bewitched* on Nickelodeon. On that show, twins were hired to play the role of baby Tabitha. But when they got older, their looks changed enough that you could tell them apart! Eventually one twin was chosen to continue playing the part.

But that didn't happen to Ashley and Mary-Kate!

Full House was a comedy about a different kind of family: Three grown men raising three little girls. Danny Tanner, played by actor Bob Saget, was the dad. Danny had just lost his wife in a car accident and was left to raise his three daughters, D.J., Stephanie, and Michelle, by himself. But he needed help. So his best friend, Joey (played by comic Dave Coulier), and brother-in-law Jesse (actor John Stamos) moved in to help out.

The three men didn't have very much in common. Danny was a television announcer, Joey was a stand-up comic and part-time inventor, and Jesse wanted to be a rock-and-roll singer. There was always something crazy going on in that household!

By the time the show began in September 1987, Ashley and Mary-Kate were already a year old. Most of their first scenes involved Michelle just being a baby. Ashley and Mary-Kate didn't have to do much. Uncle Joey would make a mess changing Michelle's diaper. Uncle Jesse would sing her a lullaby. Michelle would try to take a few steps.

The *Full House* Years

As the producers worked more and more with Mary-Kate and Ashley, they saw what special talents each of them could bring to the show. Although they looked alike, each twin had a distinct personality. "The girls could play so many different emotions because Ashley and Mary-Kate were so different," says their mom.

Once the producers realized that, it was easy to decide which twin would play which scene. In the early years, baby Ashley handled the sensitive scenes. Mary-Kate got the scenes where Michelle needed to be tough and sassy. As the girls' personalities developed, so did their roles. "Ashley became more serious, so she was given the serious lines," says their mom. "When they needed someone to be more active or emotional, they let Mary-Kate do it."

As infants, the girls sometimes needed acting

DID YOU KNOW?
- The Tanner address is 1882 Gerard Street.
- All of the Tanner kids attended Frasier Street Elementary School.
- Michelle's birthday is in November.
- Jesse's last name was Cochran, but in the fourth season he changed it to his family's Greek name, Katsopolis.

help. A cookie was often held in front of them so they would smile or giggle for the camera. And the girls' funny reactions helped make the show popular. When Mary-Kate and Ashley could finally speak, they learned their lines by mimicking their acting coach. The girls really impressed their coach because they were always willing to try something new. And they never said no to her. When they were old enough to read, they read and memorized their lines just like the other actors.

Baby Michelle was a hit! People were saying there was something special about *Full House*. Never before had a show dared to give a baby such a big part, week after week. But this time Mary-Kate and Ashley made it possible.

More and more people tuned in to see the show—and the amazing Michelle Tanner. And after a couple of seasons *Full House* became one of the top ten shows on television!

"I think it was the first time anyone really had a chance to watch a baby grow up on television," says the girls' mom. "They captured the audience's hearts."

Full House's Uncle Joey, actor Dave Coulier, agrees: "I think Mary-Kate and Ashley quickly grabbed a large piece of the audience by being really cute and by having their little catchphrases like 'You got it, dude,' and 'No way, José.'"

Viewers were thrilled that Michelle was played by twins. The show hyped the fact by having Ashley and Mary-Kate appear opposite each other. Two Michelles would sometimes appear together in a dream. Once, Michelle even met her look-alike cousin from Greece.

The girls were unaware of all the excitement around them. They never realized how popular they were. Every day Mary-Kate and Ashley just looked forward to going to the Warner Bros. Studios lot in Burbank, California, to see their "family" of coworkers. "The lot and the set were like a second home to us," says Mary-Kate.

The girls had fun playing with their young costars and with the golden retriever who played Comet. Jodie Sweetin and some of the kid guest stars would often visit Mary-Kate and Ashley in their dressing room. The girls got to decorate the room the way they wanted. It was full of games and art supplies. They often watched videos of classic musicals such as *Oklahoma!*, *Guys and Dolls*, *My Fair Lady*, and *West Side Story*.

It's no wonder that Ashley and Mary-Kate went on to star in so many musical videos of their own.

Mary-Kate and Ashley: Our Story

Going to the studio was a comfortable experience for them. "We grew up around all the people on *Full House*," says Mary-Kate. "That's what made it so much fun for us to go to work every day. We didn't do it because we had to. We did it because we loved it." The girls even complained about not working on Saturdays.

As Mary-Kate and Ashley got older, the show began featuring episodes that mirrored what was

---

DID YOU KNOW?
- The Tanners' phone number is 555-2424.
- D.J.'s private phone number is 555-8722.
- Michelle's middle name is Elizabeth.
- Tahj Mowry, who played Michelle's friend, Teddy, is the younger brother of twins Tia and Tamera Mowry from *Sister Sister*.

---

really happening in their lives: Starting kindergarten. Learning to read. Riding a bicycle for the first time. Playing soccer. Dancing. Even Mary-Kate's love of horses was written into the story when Michelle took up riding.

As the series continued, Mary-Kate and Ashley's talent shone even brighter. "We were delighted," says their producer. "As they grew up they were learning from the very talented comedians on the show. And they began acting on their own very early. Mary-Kate and Ashley weren't having lines fed to them. They were studying acting and taking classes and becoming very good actresses."

Mary-Kate and Ashley don't have much time these days to watch television. But every once in a while they'll catch an old rerun of *Full House* on the cable station Nick at Nite. Like lots of actors, Ashley and Mary-Kate don't really enjoy watching themselves on screen. They are their own toughest critics. "Sometimes we look at what we did back then and think we could have done it better," Mary-Kate admits. *Full House* fans may not agree.

After eight years the show finally came to an end in 1995. But eight years is a great success in television. In fact, *Full House* is one of ABC's longest-running comedies ever!

There's an extra bonus for Mary-Kate and Ashley and their family. They have an incredible video collection of the sisters growing up, and they didn't even have to break out their own video camera!

Mary-Kate and Ashley still miss working on *Full House*. They especially miss their TV family. "It's sad not being with the 'other family' we grew up with," says Mary-Kate. So Ashley and Mary-Kate do try to stay in touch with the *Full House* bunch. They all get together for special events. Ashley and Mary-Kate attended baby showers for their costars Candace Cameron Bure (D.J.) and Lori Loughlin (Rebecca). And they were also at the wedding of John Stamos (Uncle Jesse), who married supermodel Rebecca Romijn. Seeing their friends is always fun, but the girls admit it sometimes makes them even more "homesick" for their *Full House* days.

After the super-successful show ended, some people thought Mary-Kate and Ashley's acting careers were over. But they were wrong! Amazing new opportunities were in store for Mary-Kate and Ashley. Their exciting careers were just beginning!

Chapter 4

From TV to Video—and Lots In Between

After starring in over twenty-five videos and nine movies, Mary-Kate and Ashley have the same, if not more, experience than many of the adults in the entertainment industry. But just how did two little girls turn into two of the most powerful people in Hollywood?

Because of their huge popularity on *Full House*, fans couldn't get enough of Mary-Kate and Ashley. Their fans wanted to see *both* of the girls acting at the same time.

Mary-Kate and Ashley each loved the idea—and that's how their first television movie was born! It was called *To Grandmother's House We Go*, and each girl had a starring role. The girls made the movie during their summer break in 1992. When it aired on TV a few months later, it was one of the most-watched movies of the season.

The experience of making their first movie is something the sisters will always treasure—especially Mary-Kate. You know how people say actors are always falling in love with their costars on the set. Well, six-year-old Mary-Kate was no different—except, of course, that the costar she fell in love with was a pony!

"She was always talking about this miniature pony named Four-by-Four," Ashley remembers with a smile. "And whenever Mary-Kate was missing, we knew exactly where to find her: in the stable grooming *her* horse."

For months afterward, when asked if she liked any boys in her school, Mary-Kate would merely grin and say, "I have a crush on Four-by-Four." One day Mary-Kate's dad even found her packing to go and visit the horse. Unfortunately, the pony lived in Vancouver, Canada—far away from the girls' home in Los Angeles.

"I had a plan," Mary-Kate says. "I was going to walk to the airport and take a plane. Don't ask me how I was going to buy a ticket. Dad found me before I figured out that part."

From TV to Video—and Lots In Between

To Grandmother's House We Go was a turning point for Ashley and Mary-Kate. The movie showed everyone that the girls were an important Hollywood team. They could play individual roles—not just share the role of the TV character Michelle Tanner. Together they would go on to make films, home videos, television specials, music albums, and even a series of books based on their video characters, the Trenchcoat Twins. And they were still just kids!

Mary-Kate and Ashley's first album, *Brother for Sale*, was a hit, too. "When we were rehearsing it, Trent would say, 'I hate that song!'" recalls Ashley.

"So I'd walk around the house saying 'My favorite song is "Brother for Sale",' especially when Trent was around," Mary-Kate remembers with a grin.

"But we love our brother," Ashley is quick to point out.

In 1993, the girls released their first music video, called simply, *Our First Video*. It featured a collection of songs from Mary-Kate and Ashley's first two albums, *Brother for Sale* and *I Am the Cute One*. The sisters worked with a dance teacher to learn dance steps for the songs. But a lot of what ended up in the final video was the girls just having a blast, jumping around and bouncing on the bed!

Our First Video was big success for Ashley and

Mary-Kate. To celebrate, they took eight of their friends to a restaurant for all the hamburgers and milkshakes they could eat—and they went in a limo.

"I remember that day," Mary-Kate says. "It was such a big deal to ride in a limousine. We were all so excited."

"I don't know," Ashley admits. "I still feel kind of special when I get to ride in a limo."

Even though Mary-Kate and Ashley made quite a splash with their music, they still wanted to act. Their second TV movie for ABC was a spooky Halloween film called *Double, Double, Toil and Trouble*.

"We had a great time making that movie," Ashley recalls, "because of all the crazy costumes we wore. Mary-Kate and I have always loved spooky stories."

The year 1994 was a big one for Mary-Kate and Ashley. The two made an appearance in the film *The Little Rascals*. The girls show up in a slumber party scene. Rent it and see if you can spot them!

Later Mary-Kate and Ashley made the TV movie, *How the West Was Fun*. "I remember being so psyched about that project because I'd get to ride a horse again."

But the big news from Mary-Kate and Ashley that year was the grand opening of the Olsen and

From TV to Video—and Lots In Between

Olsen Mystery Agency. They got to play detectives in *The Adventures of Mary-Kate & Ashley*, a series of mystery videos. Nicknamed the "Trenchcoat Twins," the two adopted the motto "Will Solve Any Crime by Dinner Time." They were helped by their basset hound sidekick, Clue. The girls investigated mysteries in lots of exciting locations. The videos were shot in a spooky amusement park, aboard a U.S. Navy destroyer, at Sea World of Florida, at a volcano in Hawaii, and at many other amazing places. "We had a blast making those videos," Ashley says. "It was like playing all the time."

Mary-Kate and Ashley fans loved *The Adventures of Mary-Kate & Ashley* videos so much that a series of books based on the videos soon followed. The books were so popular that a new series of books was created called *The New Adventures of Mary-Kate & Ashley*. These books aren't based on the videos. They are all-new, original mysteries for the Trenchcoat Twins to solve.

Ashley and Mary-Kate are involved in the writing of each book. "We meet with the editors and tell them things we like to do," says Mary-Kate. "I like to horseback ride, so there is a horseback riding adventure. We both like to surf, so there's a surfing book. And Ashley likes ballet, so we did a ballet story." Today Mary-Kate and Ashley have a total of *six* different book series in bookstores!

Mary-Kate and Ashley's videos are created the same way the books are created. The girls' real lives are turned into fun, musical stories. That's how their second series of videos, *You're Invited to Mary-Kate & Ashley's*, came about. The girls loved to throw parties for their friends. By making these videos, they could share the fun with their fans.

The girls began with one of their favorite parties, *Sleepover Party*, and then the parties started getting bigger. They learned how to surf for their *Hawaiian Beach Party* and how to ski for their *Christmas Party*.

In 1995, something really big happened to Ashley and Mary-Kate. They got to star in their very first feature film! Now you could see them in your neighborhood movie theater *and* on TV! The movie was called *It Takes Two*, and in it the girls played identical "strangers," one rich and one poor. When they discover each other, they come up with a scheme to make their guardians fall in love. The movie was a huge favorite and is in video stores.

For Mary-Kate and Ashley, one of the best things about making videos and movies is that they get to travel to really exciting places. One of their family's favorite vacation spots is Hawaii. So guess what? In

1996, the entire family went on a Hawaiian surf-and-sun vacation while Mary-Kate and Ashley made some videos there!

"We made four videos that vacation," Ashley recalls. *"You're Invited to Mary-Kate & Ashley's Hawaiian Beach Party, The Case Of The Hotel Who-Done-It, The Case Of The Volcano Mystery,* and *The Case Of The U.S. Navy Adventure."*

"My favorite was *Hotel Who-Done-It,*" Mary-Kate remembers. "I was really into candy back then, and our hotel refrigerator was stocked full. We had to eat it all for the video. In real life, anything you eat gets added to your hotel bill, but this time it was free! I was in total heaven."

"I'll never forget the video we did after Hawaii," Ashley says. "It was called *The Case Of The U.S. Space Camp Mission,* and we had to wear fake teeth!"

This video was shot at a real U.S. space camp in Huntsville, Alabama. At the time of the shoot, nine-year-olds Mary-Kate and Ashley were both missing a few of their teeth. So the gaps wouldn't show on video, the girls each used fake front teeth called "flippers." But when they left home for U.S. Space Camp, they left their "teeth" on their bathroom counter.

"We wound up running around Huntsville looking for a dentist to make our emergency flippers!"

Mary-Kate remembers. "Luckily, we found someone to help us get our teeth in place just in time!"

Still, false teeth or not, to this day Mary-Kate and Ashley say that filming *The Case Of The U.S. Space Camp Mission* was one of the most thrilling experiences in their careers. When they made the video, they actually attended the space camp in Huntsville. "Trent, Dad, Ashley, and I went to a weekend parent-child session," says Mary-Kate. "We were each given different assignments to plan and carry out on a pretend space shuttle mission. We also got to work at mission control, build and launch model rockets 400 feet high, and operate shuttle simulators. Trent loves video games, so he really went wild!"

The highlight of Mary-Kate and Ashley's U.S. Space Camp experience was having dinner with a famous astronaut, Alan Bean. Alan Bean was the fourth astronaut to walk on the moon during the *Apollo XII* mission in 1970. (*Apollo XII* was the second spaceship to land on the moon.) "We felt so honored to have dinner with one of only twelve people on Earth who have ever touched the moon," says Ashley.

"I'll never forget that evening," Mary-Kate recalls. "Even though we were just young kids, he answered all our questions and made us understand what it was like to travel in space."

For the video, the girls suited up as astronauts. Then they rode in space simulators, where they could experience how it would really feel to walk on the moon. "It was a strange sensation," says Mary-Kate. "Half walking, half floating."

Even though she loved working in Hawaii and at space camp, Ashley's favorite video is no surprise: *Ballet Party*, with the New York City Ballet! Finally, she had a chance to show off her dancing talent. "I got to live out one of my big dreams," says Ashley. "We had to practice with a choreographer for days before the actual shoot. Because I had taken dance lessons for so long, I had a pretty good idea of what the steps were. But you should have seen Mary-Kate!"

Mary-Kate admits she was a bit nervous about getting up on stage—especially since the other girls in the video were students at a famous performing arts school called The Juilliard School. But Mary-Kate held her own.

"Whether you're a dancer or an athlete, you have to have a lot of strength and coordination," Ashley says. "Well, Mary-Kate had both. She worked really hard at all those pliés and jetés, and she was great. I think she surprised everyone, especially herself."

Mary-Kate had the upper hand for their next video. *Camp Out Party* was right in Mary-Kate's neck of the woods! Sleeping in a tent. Hiking in fresh air. Fishing and roasting marshmallows. "Not a few of Ashley's favorite things," Mary-Kate teases, "but we managed to get her there anyhow."

Whether it was dancing on their toes, going on a space mission, or skiing in the Rockies, Mary-Kate and Ashley were willing to give anything a try. Their fans around the world couldn't wait to see what they tried next.

Mary-Kate and Ashley would not disappoint them. In 1998, the sisters released their first *ninety-minute* direct-to-video movie called *Billboard Dad*. Again, Mary-Kate and Ashley got to do things they enjoy in real life. Mary-Kate played Tess, a surfer, and Ashley played Emily, a high diver. In the story, the girls teamed up to find a new love for their single dad—by placing an ad on a billboard!

Billboard Dad was the first of many full-length direct-to-video movies that Mary-Kate and Ashley would star in—movies that their fans would enjoy again and again.

Chapter 5

Shining Stars

Lights! Camera! Action!

Billboard Dad was great fun to make, and Ashley and Mary-Kate discovered that the change from a thirty-minute video to a ninety-minute video was triple the fun.

But it was hard work, too. It takes much more time to learn all the dialogue and shoot all the scenes and much more planning to get all the details—sets, lighting, wardrobe, and so on—just right! And when you're the executive producers of a film as well as the stars—as Mary-Kate and Ashley are—it's a lot of responsibility. But Mary-Kate and Ashley welcomed the challenge, and they always found a way to mix hard work with fun!

"In *Passport to Paris* I played Melanie and Ashley played Allison," Mary-Kate explains. "We're sent to stay with our grandfather in Paris, France, during spring break." Of course, it wouldn't be any fun if the girls didn't get into mischief while seeing the sights of the city . . . or while riding around Paris on motor scooters with cute boys!

Well, that part was fun, but another part of the movie proved to be a bit more challenging.

Ashley was supposed to speak some French in the movie. So when the girls got to Paris, they both decided to speak the language whenever they could. Their French tutor traveled with them, and they experimented on their own. They did their best to order in French while dining out. Once they were even daring enough to try *escargots*—snails! Snails are a delicacy in France. Ashley thought they were *"très bon,"* while Mary-Kate made it clear in English that she didn't care for the dish: "Yuck!"

But what really took guts for Mary-Kate and Ashley came in the boy department. *Passport to Paris* was their first romantic comedy. At thirteen they were each going to have their first screen kiss—and they would have to pull it off with a crew of fifty people standing around watching! And on the very first day they met the boys! Talk about pressure! The girls admit they were a little shy about having their first kisses in front of an audience. But they got plenty of chances to get used to it: They had to do it several times to get it just right for the camera!

"If you want to make movies," Mary-Kate says, "you can't be afraid of being embarrassed. You have to do your job in front of a group of people. So you have to be ready to put yourself out there."

Big crowds are nothing new when you're on the set of a Mary-Kate and Ashley movie. In *Holiday in the Sun*, the girls play Madison and Alex, who stumble across a smuggling ring in the Bahamas. It was filmed at the beautiful Atlantis resort on Paradise Island. Since the movie was shot in the summer, there were lots of families staying at the hotel, and that meant crowds of Mary-Kate and Ashley fans everywhere. Ashley and Mary-Kate were recognized wherever they went.

"Sometimes we were late to the set," Ashley recalls, "because we kept stopping to say hello and to sign autographs."

"I remember once when the producer picked me up from my room so that I wouldn't stop to talk to our fans," Mary-Kate says. "He suggested I wear a big hat and sunglasses so that I wouldn't be recognized, but I didn't think it would work."

And it didn't. The fans recognized Mary-Kate at once. The minute she and the producer entered the lobby, a bunch of girls came over and screamed out, "Hi, Mary-Kate!" This was especially funny since several of the crew members on the set still couldn't tell Mary-Kate and Ashley apart.

One time that Mary-Kate and Ashley were *not* recognized was when they were filming *When in Rome.* In this movie, Mary-Kate and Ashley played Charli and Leila, two girls who become interns in the fashion department of a big Italian company.

"My character, Charli, had a crush on an Italian boy named Paolo," Mary-Kate says. "Paolo was played by Michaelangelo Tomasso, a famous actor in Italy. One day, when we were shooting a romantic scene in Rome, a group of Italian girls asked if they could take a picture with Michaelangelo—and they asked me to step away so I wouldn't be in the picture!"

"Sometimes when we're shooting on location we need to film a scene without any people in the background. This happened a few times during our shoot for *Winning London.* We got to go into Westminster Abbey before it opened," Ashley says. "It was an amazing feeling being in such a historic church." Westminster Abbey is more than nine hundred years old, and most of England's kings and queens were crowned there. It is also the burial place for many important people in England's history, such as the famous author Charles Dickens, poet Robert Browning, and scientists Sir Isaac Newton and Charles Darwin.

DID YOU KNOW?
In *Winning London*, the boy who plays the English character, James, isn't English? He's Australian!

"It was also fun shooting at the Tower of London— until our time ran out!" Ashley tells us. "The security guards made us put away our cameras and stop filming. But to get just a little more, the director whipped out his home movie camera and shot as we were leaving. The video footage is in the movie!"

"Being on a movie location is like being with a great big family," Mary-Kate says. "You get very close with the people you work with."

Winning London was about kids from all around the world, coming together to debate in the model United Nations. "It was a competition," Ashley says. "Our team was from the United States, and we were all supposed to be friends. And that's exactly what happened—in real life."

"It wasn't hard to imagine being good friends with these kids," Mary-Kate recalls. "There was a group of five of us. We had a blast!"

Mary-Kate and Ashley also have a special place in their hearts for their movie, *Holiday in the Sun*. The movie was shot in the summer, so Ashley and Mary-Kate didn't have to worry about school. "We had so much fun playing on the beach and hanging out by the pool!" Mary-Kate remembers. "We all just clicked, you know. By the end of filming the group was really tight. I had a feeling that we'd stay in touch back home. I'm glad I was right."

"The cast and crew of a movie are all there to support one another," Ashley says. "So we don't have to be afraid to make mistakes."

"And there have been lots of them!" Mary-Kate laughs.

Passport to Paris was shot half in Paris and half in Los Angeles. All of the outside shots were done in Paris. Weeks later, the inside shots were filmed in a movie studio in Los Angeles. This worked fine for most of the movie, but if you look closely you can see a problem in one scene—the one where they are saying good-bye to everyone at the embassy.

Most of the scene was shot inside (in Los

Angeles). But then everyone walks outside (shot in Paris). To make it work, the clothes had to be the same in both parts of the scene. But when they shipped the clothes from France to California, the dress that the character Bridget wore got lost. They had to try to make another dress. If you look very closely, you can see that the dresses are not exactly alike.

Getting There is about two girls who recently get their driver's licenses and take a road trip to the winter Olympics in Utah. There was a lot of skiing in that movie and one of the characters, Lindi, breaks her leg. "But that was never supposed to happen," Mary-Kate admits. "The actress who played Lindi had an accident while they were shooting and really did break her leg."

"That was a problem because now that she had a cast on her leg, she couldn't do some of the scenes that were in the script," Ashley says.

So what did they do?

They changed the story so that Lindi breaks her leg and that way the actress could continue with the movie!

But a problem isn't always that easy to fix. Sometimes you encounter things you can't do anything about. "One time when we were shooting a movie,

Mary-Kate got the giggles during a very serious scene," Ashley remembers. "She was laughing so hard that we had to stop shooting and take a break. After Mary-Kate calmed down we started shooting again. I turned to my sister and asked, 'Are you okay now?' and then *I* started laughing!"

"Soon the entire crew was laughing," adds Mary-Kate. "It took about twenty minutes to get everyone calmed down and quiet."

But Mary-Kate and Ashley admit that their toughest problem occurred in *The Challenge*. Why? Because nearly everyone on the set got sick from the water in Mexico! "They call it Montezuma's Revenge," Mary-Kate says. "It's kind of funny, now that I can look back on it. You know, since the video is called *The Challenge*."

But you never see any of the problems on film. That's the magic of the movies.

Problems or not, Mary-Kate and Ashley are always ready to jump in when the director yells "action"—and we mean ACTION!

In *Holiday in the Sun*, Mary-Kate and Ashley were the first ones to hop on jet skis, swoosh down a huge slide, or swim with the dolphins. In *Winning London* they learned how to play polo and how to fence!

Our Lips Are Sealed followed Mary-Kate and

Ashley as they unsuccessfully tried to hide out from bad guys in Australia. Mary-Kate and Ashley marveled at how beautiful the country was and loved shooting a movie "down under."

"It took fourteen hours to get there, but it was so worth it," Ashley says. "We got to do a lot of surfing in that movie. We learned how to do it from a champion surfer!"

The stunts in *Our Lips Are Sealed* weren't always so easy. One time they had to work with a kangaroo.

"Vince the kangaroo was so cuddly and friendly, Ashley and I just wanted to take him home," remembers Mary-Kate.

Too bad they couldn't. Mary-Kate and Ashley shot only part of *Our Lips Are Sealed* in Australia. The other part was filmed in a Los Angeles movie studio. When Mary-Kate and Ashley returned home to finish shooting the rest of the movie they had to work with a different kangaroo—only this kangaroo wasn't nearly as friendly as Vince. In fact, he was kind of crabby!

"We were a little nervous doing our scenes around the new kangaroo, but we were very professional about it. We got through it as fast as we could, and then it was *See you later!*" Ashley says.

The next time you watch *Our Lips Are Sealed*, see

Mary-Kate and Ashley's Surfing Lingo

Wipeout: When you are thrown off the board into the ocean.

Over the falls: A wipeout when the wave crashes over you and you are thrown up over it, like going over a waterfall.

Tubed: Surfing inside the wave, under the curl.

Stoked: Feeling excited about the waves!

Floater: When you board up to the lip of the wave and float down while you ride the board.

Off the lip: When you are on the very top of the wave, you go through the edge of the wave and it forces you down.

Got the fever: Feeling like you have to go out and surf!

if you can tell the difference between Vince and the other kangaroo!

Another time during *Our Lips Are Sealed* Ashley and Mary-Kate had to walk on top of the famous Sydney bridge that crosses Sydney harbor. It's very high and very scary. But the worst part was when a thunderstorm was breaking out in the distance while Mary-Kate and Ashley were up there. The girls had to get off that bridge fast or risk being hit by lightning!

Shining Stars

Mary-Kate and Ashley had to cross another bridge in one of their more recent movies, *The Challenge*. This bridge was hung over jagged rocks, and it was made of rope. It was the kind of bridge that sways from side to side when you cross it, and it can flip over! And Mary-Kate and Ashley's characters had to cross it in order to win a *Survivor*-type competition.

"The crew was nervous about us walking the bridge—even with the safety harnesses," Ashley recalls. "But Mary-Kate and I were up for it."

Another "challenge" involved balancing on a tall telephone pole that was standing out in the ocean. "The top of the pole was about the size of a plate," Ashley remembers. "And I had to stand on it for almost an hour without falling into the water."

There are times when you *think* you're seeing something in a movie, but it's really a fake. For example, in a scene from *The Challenge*, Mary-Kate has to eat worms. And it really looks like she is!

Yes, Mary-Kate had to dip her hand into a gross plate of real worms. But when you see her eat one, it's only a brown Gummi Worm.

Mary-Kate throws a boomerang perfectly in *Our Lips Are Sealed*. It always comes right back to her. How did she manage to do this? More movie magic.

Mary-Kate threw the boomerang, but then the film-makers used computer imaging to show the boomerang going just where it had to go.

In *Billboard Dad*, the girls paint a giant billboard on Sunset Boulevard in Los Angeles. It wouldn't be safe to do that for real—so high up with traffic below. So the filmmakers made a small billboard on a soundstage, then they shot the scene with a plain green screen in the background. Later, through the magic of movies, they inserted Sunset Boulevard in the background.

In *Getting There*, Mary-Kate and Ashley had to drive a car, but they had only learner's permits. That meant they needed an adult in the car with them when they were driving, but the scenes they were shooting didn't call for an adult to be in the car. What did they do? That's right—more movie magic! Off camera, the car was towed. On camera, it looked as if Ashley and Mary-Kate were actually driving!

As Mary-Kate and Ashley get older, their movies reflect the changes in their lifestyles. That's why independence is such a strong theme in *Getting There*. In this movie, Mary-Kate and Ashley play girls who are about to take their first road trip—to the winter Olympics in Utah!

"*Getting There* was a little closer to home for us,

and I don't mean because it was made in the United States," Mary-Kate says. "It reflects our real life in a way. At the time we made the movie, Ashley and I were just learning how to drive ourselves."

"Yeah," Ashley agrees. "We wanted to get in as much driving time as possible. We still do."

Mary-Kate and Ashley like to make movies that are fun for them to do—and just as fun for you to watch. Now that Ashley and Mary-Kate are older, they are much more involved in the "behind the scenes" action of their movies than they were when they were kids. "We love acting," Ashley points out, "but it's just as important to know what to look for from behind the camera as it is to know what your character is all about."

Now, as executive producers of their movies, Mary-Kate and Ashley not only pick the locations, they help the other producers and the writers come up with cool stories. "They'll give us a bunch of ideas and we'll tell them what we like and what we don't like," Ashley says. "And sometimes the writers will work from ideas that we come up with."

Mary-Kate and Ashley also play a big role in the writing of their scripts. "We want to make sure that our movies are entertaining," Mary-Kate says.

To do that, they give the writers their comments

on scripts and the writers make changes. A script has to get the okay from Mary-Kate and Ashley before production on a movie can begin. In addition, Ashley and Mary-Kate are very involved in casting, and they work with the other producers to choose actors for their movies. They also decide which songs will be used for their movie soundtracks.

On top of all that, Mary-Kate and Ashley play a role behind the camera. Many times, after Ashley or Mary-Kate acts in a scene, they will watch it on a monitor to make sure the scene is right. They'll make comments like "That was good!" or "I can do better. Let's try it again."

"It's great experience," Ashley admits, "since we'd like to try directing one day."

Until then, Ashley and Mary-Kate have their hands full. In 2003, they released what is scheduled to be their final direct-to-video movie—*The Challenge*. But don't worry, Mary-Kate and Ashley won't be going away. They're moving on to the big screen!

The Challenge was filmed in Cabo San Lucas, Mexico. It's about a group of kids who are in a teen *Survivor*-type game, competing for college scholarships. Mary-Kate and Ashley play sisters who do *not* like each other. Their parents are divorced and one girl lives with their father in Washington while the other lives with their mother in Los Angeles.

Unfortunately, they get put on the same team with a group of other kids, and Mary-Kate and Ashley are constantly fighting. They have to learn to work together or they'll blow it for everybody. Of course they learn to get along with each other by the end of the movie!

"It was a nice twist on the roles Mary-Kate and I usually play," Ashley says. "It was kind of fun to have a conflict between us."

"I really liked the *Survivor* aspect of the whole thing," Mary-Kate says. "And there's a cool surprise at the end," she adds. "But I don't want to give it away. You'll have to see it for yourself!"

What's next for Mary-Kate and Ashley? Well, they're working on making a major feature film for Warner Bros. Studios!

"We were at a crossroads in our careers," Ashley says. "We had to decide if we wanted to keep doing the same thing or if we wanted to try something new."

"And we chose to go for it!" Mary-Kate adds.

Chapter 6

Television for Two

Mary-Kate and Ashley Olsen. Also known as Michelle Tanner. Also known as Mary-Kate and Ashley Burke. Also known as Chloe and Riley Carlson. Also known as Special Agents Misty and Amber. In four different series Ashley and Mary-Kate have always been favorites on television.

When *Full House* ended, the sisters got busy with videos and movies. But in 1998, they were ready to return to TV. They starred in an ABC television series called *TWO of a kind*.

The show was about twin girls named Mary-Kate and Ashley! But instead of Olsen, their last name was Burke. "Our characters were opposites," Mary-Kate says. "The producers took some of our own personality differences and exaggerated them. I played a tomboy whose biggest interest was perfecting her curveball. Ashley played a straight-A student who was starting to like boys."

"I'm not as girlie in real life as I was on the show," Ashley says. And Mary-Kate agrees, "I'm not as sporty or tomboyish as my character. But the differences between the two characters made the show really funny."

The make-believe Burke family lived in Chicago with their single dad, a college professor. He was on the hunt for a baby-sitter to watch the girls after school and be a good role model.

Actor Christopher Seiber played Mary-Kate and Ashley's dad. The baby-sitter was played by Sally Wheeler. This was Chris and Sally's big television break. They would be working with seasoned pros Mary-Kate and Ashley, who had already been in show business for twelve years.

"On the first day I was terribly nervous," admits Sally. "I went up to the girls and said, 'Well, you guys, you know I've never actually done something like this. I'm so nervous.' And they said, 'Hey, don't worry. You can always do the scene again if you mess up. Come on, calm down.' Mary-Kate and Ashley were so generous and very helpful."

Sally found that she had a lot in common with Mary-Kate and Ashley. Like Mary-Kate, Sally had a passion for horses. And like both girls, Sally enjoyed Rollerblading. The three of them could often be found skating around the Warner Bros. Studios lot.

After the first episode, or "pilot," was completed, Mary-Kate spoke up. She wanted her character to have a softer look. "She looked like a total tomboy," Mary-Kate said. "They kept bringing me out in a football or basketball uniform. I didn't really like that, so we changed it. My character was still a tomboy who liked to hang out with the guys. She loved to play football and basketball, but the way she dressed was a little different." Instead of sports jerseys, Mary-Kate got to wear jeans on the show. Ashley usually wore a dressier outfit. "That's definitely her style in real life," says Mary-Kate.

Unfortunately, *TWO of a kind* lasted only one season in its first run. "We were sad that it came to an end," says Ashley, "because for a season you kind of get attached to the people you're working with. But it wasn't like the end of *Full House*. *Full House* was something very special."

Two years later Ashley and Mary-Kate were back with *So Little Time* on the Fox Family channel (now ABC Family). But this television project was different from the others. This time Mary-Kate and Ashley were executive producers of their show. Not only did the sisters help come up with the idea, they were involved in lots of different ways, from scripts to casting to wardrobe. They became the first teens to produce and star in their own television series!

And it wasn't easy. *So Little Time* had a hectic schedule. Usually a weekly television show finishes filming one episode in about five days. Mary-Kate and Ashley shot more than one episode in *four* days.

Mary-Kate played Riley Carlson and Ashley starred as her sister, Chloe. "Our characters were more sophisticated than the Burke sisters," explains Mary-Kate. "Riley is into nature and saving the world. She's very spontaneous and no two days are alike for her. Chloe, on the other hand, is a creature of habit. She plays the mommy's girl, who is totally high-strung and a definite overachiever."

If the character names sound familiar, then you probably remember them from *Winning London*. They liked the names so much they wanted to use them again. But just to keep you on your toes, the sisters decided to swap! In the movie, Mary-Kate played Chloe while Ashley played Riley.

The show's theme song also appeared in *Winning London*. "So Little Time" is performed by the British group Arcana and actually inspired the name of the television series!

On the show, on top of having normal teenage troubles, Riley and Chloe had to deal with the separation of their parents. Their mom, Macy, was a high-powered fashion designer living in a Malibu beach home. Their dad, Jake, was trying to "find himself" and moved into a tiny trailer nearby. Chloe and Riley lived with their mom but saw their dad all the time.

With both *TWO of a kind* and *So Little Time*, Ashley and Mary-Kate had to divide their day between work and school. They worked four days a week. Every morning they studied with their studio teachers for three hours. Their schoolwork at the studio matched the work their classmates were doing back at Mary-Kate and Ashley's regular school.

The sisters made twenty-six episodes of *So Little Time* but chose not to continue. They had made a deal with Warner Bros. to star in a feature film before they started college. To accomplish this, Mary-Kate and Ashley had to take a break from TV in 2002.

Ironically, that same year, Mary-Kate received a nomination for a Daytime Emmy Award as "Outstanding Performer in a Children's Series." Even though she didn't win the gold statuette, it was still a great honor just to be considered.

Television for Two

Check out your cable stations for reruns of *TWO of a kind* and *So Little Time* on the ABC Family network.

And you can also see Mary-Kate and Ashley in animation on Nickelodeon. In 2001 they executive-produced and starred in the cartoon show *Mary-Kate and Ashley in ACTION!*

In this series Mary-Kate supplies the voice of Special Agent Misty while Ashley plays Special Agent Amber, two hip teens who travel the world to fight crime and supervillains. While the Trenchcoat Twins had their basset hound sidekick Clue, Misty and Amber are aided by the fluffy white Quincy—a computerized canine who can talk!

"We spent a lot of time with the artists and writers to create this show," Mary-Kate says. "It took a real team effort to develop just the right look for Misty and Amber."

"And it was a new challenge, acting with only our voices," Ashley adds. "We're really happy with how it turned out."

While Mary-Kate and Ashley are now working on a big-screen career, they'll always remember the fun they had on their television series.

"It's where we got our start," Ashley says. "It's where we grew up."

Chapter 7

The *mary-kateandashley* Brand

The music pulses as models prance down the runway in hot fashions for teens. The cameras flash as photographers take picture after picture of the newest *mary-kateandashley* brand clothes and accessories. And after the last model completes her walk, Mary-Kate and Ashley bound down the runway together. The cameras flash again, capturing them in their fabulous business suits.

Why are they wearing business suits? Because Mary-Kate and Ashley are not only fantastic actresses, they're savvy businesswomen, too. Their apparel is the coolest thing in the stores.

But the *mary-kateandashley* brand fashion line didn't just happen overnight. At the age of ten, the sisters began working with executive designer, Judy Swartz. She would plan their outfits for their video and public appearances. The girls admit that they needed some help when it came to clothes back then. "I had my favorite shorts that I never took off," recalls Mary-Kate. "They were tight Spandex with fringe."

"She would wear those every day!" Ashley laughs. "And I only wore baggy clothes. We were pretty bad before Judy."

When Ashley and Mary-Kate did the TV series *TWO of a kind*, Judy was asked to put together the wardrobe for the show. Like other twelve-year-olds, Mary-Kate and Ashley wanted to look older and more sophisticated. To accomplish that, Judy bought them adult clothes and had them cut down to fit.

The unique look was a hit and fans wanted to know where they could get cool clothes like Ashley and Mary-Kate's. With Judy's design expertise, the sisters launched the *mary-kateandashley* brand of clothing at Wal-Mart stores across the country in early 2001.

The first season of clothes featured 1970s-inspired peasant blouses, tank tops, jeans, shoes, sleepwear, jewelry, and sunglasses. "Sometimes the fashion line is influenced by the clothes in our movies," Mary-Kate tells us.

"But mostly it's inspired by the fashions we wear and like," Ashley adds.

And what would a fashion line be without a grand runway show? Mary-Kate and Ashley showed off their new designs with a fun runway show and party in Hollywood. The fashion show was called Mary-Kate and Ashley Fashion Forward, and it was cybercast on AOL and aired on the Fox Family channel in the United States (now ABC Family).

The *mary-kateandashley* brand fashion line quickly became one of the fastest growing 'tween and teen clothing lines in America. Wal-Mart couldn't keep the items in stock! They sold out in a matter of weeks.

Mary-Kate and Ashley quickly got back into action to expand their clothing line. They play a big part in the design of each piece that is produced. "We're very involved in picking the clothing we want to see next season," says Ashley. "Judy will go to the fashion capitals of the world to look for new trends. Sometimes she'll find them at a fashion show. Other times she'll spot a guy or girl wearing an interesting outfit on the street."

"Then she'll come back to us with several trends

she thinks are going to be big," Mary-Kate says. "We'll tell her which ones we want to go with."

"Or sometimes we'll get inspired by something and come up with our own design idea and take it from there," Ashley adds.

"I work very closely with Mary-Kate and Ashley throughout the entire process," Judy points out. "I show them designs, fabrics, and samples of finished products. They'll give me their opinions at every stage. Sometimes we'll need to make small changes. Other times we'll decide that a particular design isn't right for the line and start over."

"We're firm about what kinds of products we'll put our names on," Mary-Kate says. "It doesn't make sense to put out something we don't like."

"It seems to be working," Ashley says. "We have gotten some great feedback about *mary-kateandashley* brand fashions from the kids who wear them."

"Mary-Kate and Ashley have great fashion intuition," Judy adds. "So far they've been right every time."

Mary-Kate and Ashley love to wear lots of accessories—bracelets, rope or beaded chokers, ankle bracelets, and all sorts of jewelry.

"I love watches," Mary-Kate says. "I can't have enough of them!" "And don't forget shoes," Ashley adds. "Especially strappy sandals and flip-flops!" In addition to a large collection of shoes, Ashley has a weakness for handbags.

Both girls have learned that the trick to looking great is feeling great. And that comes from having a good diet and getting plenty of exercise. Ashley and Mary-Kate both stay active with yoga. And they eat lots of fruits, salad, and fish. The girls aren't really interested in candy anymore. And instead of soda, they'll usually reach for juice or water.

"I do have one big weakness," Mary-Kate admits. "It's gum. I'll stuff five pieces in my mouth if no one is looking!"

Having a successful clothing line was something the girls once only dreamed about. "We love fashion and thought a lot about having a clothing line when we got older," says Ashley. "And now it's really happening."

Over time the line has grown to include cosmetics, handbags, accessories, fragrances, shampoo, and sheets and comforters. In 2003 *mary-kateandashley* brand fashions spread around the globe. Now they are available in various stores in countries such as Australia, the United Kingdom, and Mexico. And soon they'll be in other countries, too!

The *mary-kateandashley* Brand

Mary-Kate and Ashley are more than just teen actors and fashion designers. They continue to have a successful line of books based on characters they've played, and in 2001 were editors-in-chief of *mary-kateandashley* magazine. *mary-kateandashley* had a more grown-up look than other teen magazines. "We covered fashion, music, movies, sports, yoga, and guys," says Mary-Kate. While the magazine was very popular, after three issues it was put on hold; the publishing company behind the magazine went out of business.

While they were disappointed about the hold on their magazine, the sisters have kept busy with other fun ventures, like their line of fashion dolls with Mattel. "It's a little weird to see yourself as a doll," admits Ashley.

In 2000, the fashion dolls looked like Mary-Kate and Ashley during their short-haired days of *TWO of a kind*. In 2002 Mattel introduced a Mary-Kate and Ashley Sweet 16 line of fashion dolls that have a more contemporary look and resemble the sisters with longer hair.

Then there's Mary-Kate and Ashley's popular line of interactive video games based on themselves. "We both thought creating video games for girls was a good idea," says Ashley. "Most video games are geared to boys, but these games are all about things girls like to do."

Their simple concept turned into a huge success. "We're happy that our fans like them," Mary-Kate says.

When the *Winners Circle* game was released, it quickly became the hottest-selling game among girls for both Game Boy and PlayStation2. The game featured the girls horseback riding.

From concept to actually playing the game once it's finished, Mary-Kate and Ashley are key advisers every step of the way. "We are involved in the whole process," says Ashley. "We're shown the game in different stages and we give our input."

Other Mary-Kate and Ashley video games have included *Magical Mystery Mall*, *The New Adventures of Mary-Kate and Ashley*, *Crush Course*, and *Get a Clue*.

Sweet 16: Licensed to Drive is their most innovative video game so far. *Sweet 16: Licensed to Drive* invites kids to join Mary-Kate and Ashley for a huge birthday bash. The party games include a challenging driver's test, rock climbing, jet skiing, surfing, and many more things that Mary-Kate and Ashley like to do in real life!

With clothes, makeup, accessories, bedding, games,

The *mary-kateandashley* Brand

and much more, the *mary-kateandashley* brand is a hit! While it may sound like a job (and it is!), Mary-Kate and Ashley are having fun and are still the same down-to-earth girls they've always been. "It's kind of hard to even say that we are a brand," says Mary-Kate. "We don't think of ourselves like that. We're just us."

Chapter 8

Past, Present, Personal

On *Full House* Michelle once got into trouble at school when she accidentally let the class bird out of its cage. But by the end of the episode, she made up for it by replacing the bird.

Real life, though, can be a little more complicated! Mary-Kate and Ashley's home life is probably a lot like yours. They sometimes have school problems, questions about boys, worries about friends. And those kinds of problems are hardly ever solved as fast as they are on TV!

Like most teens, Mary-Kate and Ashley have to listen to their parents. They have curfews and rules that they need to follow.

Mary-Kate and Ashley's parents are careful not

to let the girls' careers get in the way of having a normal family and social life. The sisters still make plenty of time to see their friends—as long as their homework gets done. It's very important that Mary-Kate and Ashley keep up their grades, no matter how busy their careers. As they approach the end of high school, grades are particularly important. They need to earn the highest grades they can to get into a great college.

"Mary-Kate and Ashley are two of the most disciplined people I know," says a producer who works with them. "They are extremely focused. Not only do they learn their lines and deal with the other aspects of acting, but they study and do homework, too. They have an excellent work ethic, which allows them to get it all done—and done well."

Like any students, though, the sisters each have classes that aren't their favorites, but they still work hard at doing the very best they can.

"Ashley and Mary-Kate give over a hundred percent to everything they do," says their dad.

Mary-Kate and Ashley go to a great school. No one makes a big deal about their being celebrities or being twins. "When we're not working we go to regular classes like everybody else," says Ashley.

"We have lots of good friends at school. We are not treated any differently."

Still, just like everyone else, they sometimes get teased. "The only thing they give us a hard time about is being petite," reveals Mary-Kate, with a grin. "We're really little," Ashley adds. "Our brother Trent says it takes two of us just to make one person." As they wrapped up their junior year of high school, Ashley was five feet one inch, and Mary-Kate was five feet.

While they may seem cool and collected on screen, the one thing that does make them nervous is performing in front of a live audience. But they still want to talk to their fans, so they don't let the nervous jitters stop them.

At the age of seven they were already speaking to 3,000 kids and parents at Walt Disney World. Later, they talked to 20,000 fans at the Mall of America in Minneapolis! And more recently, they were award presenters at the live MTV Music Video Awards with thousands of fans and millions of television viewers around the world cheering them on.

Yes, they do a great job in front of crowds, but they still get butterflies in their stomachs—just like when you stand up in front of your class at school to give a speech.

Past, Present, Personal

Mary-Kate and Ashley don't have any problem at all making movies. If they need to film a scene over again, they do. It's all edited later and any mistakes the girls make get left out. But it's different when they appear on a talk show, like *The Tonight Show*. "You can't do it again if you mess up," says Mary-Kate. Through practice, though, the girls are getting over their fear of appearing live. "We do a lot of deep breathing beforehand," says Mary-Kate. "That usually helps."

As teens, the girls find new challenges to tackle such as taking their driving tests, applying to colleges, and, of course, boys. Through school and friends, Mary-Kate and Ashley are meeting guys, and dating.

What kind of guy makes a good boyfriend? They both like independent guys who can think for themselves. "He has to be funny, cute, and nice. And he can't whine a lot," says Mary-Kate. Ashley likes guys who are smart, driven, and motivated, as well as "funny and cute—and not clingy!" Do we even need to mention that Ashley has to approve of the guys Mary-Kate wants to date, and vice versa? They do, of course!

For Mary-Kate and Ashley's sixteenth birthday, they went on a double date they would remember for the rest of their lives. They were taken to their favorite restaurant for dinner. What they didn't know was that inside would be eighty of their friends, family, and coworkers waiting to yell, "Surprise!" Their sweet sixteen party featured a photo booth, a Tarot card reader, dancing, and a lot of fun! They each got a birthday cake decorated to look like a California driver's license—complete with their pictures on it!

So far the guys they've dated haven't been in show business, but the girls do have show biz friends. Prince of pop Aaron Carter counts himself as one of their admirers. "I'll tell you the truth, I love the Olsen twins," Aaron admits.

As Ashley and Mary-Kate get older, they're beginning to develop a very sophisticated style. They've been photographed for many magazines—*Vogue*, *Vanity Fair*, *Women's Wear Daily*, and *People*, to name a few of the hundreds they've been in.

So what's next? As they've grown up, Mary-Kate and Ashley's ideas about what they'd like to do in the future sure have changed. Now that the girls are teenagers, a whole new world of choices awaits them.

Will they go to college as planned?

Continue to act?

Move to careers behind the camera?

Continue to be fashion designers?

It's all possible! Mary-Kate and Ashley have proved they are talented in show business, the fashion business, *and* in school. There's no reason they can't do it all!

The sisters are currently waiting to see which colleges accept them. They want to attend school together, preferably on the East Coast, which would be far from home but close to one of their favorite cities, New York City.

They will likely study both business and theater. Ashley loves the business side of things while Mary-Kate leans toward the creative side. Mary-Kate is also interested in taking courses in photography and cooking. She plans to keep up her riding while away at school. Both girls hope to spend a semester studying abroad, possibly in Italy.

Mary-Kate and Ashley are also working on a feature film for their own production company and Warner Bros. and are looking very carefully at how their movie characters are developed. The roles they want to play are a bit more grown-up. "We might want to try something a little more dramatic," Ashley says.

"But we wouldn't rule out an action movie," adds

Mary-Kate. "Car chases. Stunts. Danger. That sounds like a lot of fun."

And there are people they would like to be able

1992

Mary-Kate: *"I want to be a candymaker and a cowgirl when I grow up."*

Ashley: *"I would like to be a candymaker and an actress. The food scenes are so much fun!"*

1994

Mary-Kate: *"I want to be an animal trainer for the movies. I want to have my own horse ranch."*

Ashley: *"I want to be a makeup artist, or I might keep acting."*

1997

Mary-Kate: *"I would like to train dolphins and whales, preferably at Sea World."*

Ashley: *"I really like acting. It's a lot of fun. And I would like to direct someday, too."*

2001

Mary-Kate: *"I see myself still acting, running our company, and horseback riding."*

Ashley: *"I want to direct, but I also want to be really active in running our company and working with our fashion line."*

---

to work with as well. "It would be great to work with Cameron Diaz or Luke Wilson," Mary-Kate says.

"I admire what Reese Witherspoon and Drew Barrymore are doing," Ashley adds. "They're on the big screen as actresses, and they're producing movies that they *don't* star in."

One thing the sisters may try someday is directing. Since they've grown up in front of a camera, they've learned the basics. They produce the movies they star in. "I can't wait to learn more about directing," Ashley says. "It's something I'd like to pursue in college."

For now, acting is still Ashley and Mary-Kate's number one interest. But if they want to give up acting and be everyday kids, that's okay. "If the girls ever decide they've had enough, that's fine," says their mom. "So far, that hasn't come close to happening."

"We would say 'We've had enough,'" Mary-Kate says, "if we wanted to quit." She turns to her sister and they both break into big grins.

"But we're not going to say it because we love doing this," Ashley adds.

The phenomenal success of Mary-Kate and Ashley stems from familiarity. "Fans feel like they're close to us because they've seen us grow up," Mary-Kate tells us. But their popularity hasn't gone to their heads.

"There are fashion dolls of us and Game Boys of us, but it doesn't really faze us," says Ashley.

When asked about what accomplishments they'll be most proud of, Ashley says, "Staying grounded while all this is going on around us." Mary-Kate adds, "Graduating from high school and going to college."

And for the near future, the two will be working and playing together on screen and off. "Maybe in the future we'll do a movie or something separately," predicts Mary-Kate. Ashley chimes in, "One day when we're a lot older, but we have no idea when that will be. Right now, we're going to have fun *together!*"

Mary-Kate and Ashley have hopes and dreams just like you. Many of their dreams are coming true. And they know how it can happen for you, too!

"If you really want to do something, go for it," advises Ashley. "Work hard and you will succeed."

MARY-KATE AND ASHLEY
FUN FACTS

•When *Full House* began, Mary-Kate's name was *not* hyphenated.

•In photographs where the girls are dressed in blue and pink or red, it's almost always Mary-Kate wearing blue and Ashley in pink or red.

•In 1993 they were Junior Grand Marshals of the holiday Christmas parade in Hollywood.

•They've made movies in the United States, England, Australia, the Bahamas, Mexico, France, and Canada.

•Mary-Kate and Ashley rode on the Jell-O float in the 1997 Macy's Thanksgiving Day parade.

•The sisters have been guests of honor on six Sail With The Stars cruises including ones to Russia, the Caribbean, and Alaska.

•Mary-Kate and Ashley were named Teen Ambassadors to the U.S. Women's World Cup soccer team in 1999, the year the team won!

•The sisters both like to fall asleep with their televisions on.

•They've starred in four television series: *Full House*, *TWO of a kind*, *So Little Time*, and *Mary-Kate and Ashley in ACTION!*

•Nickelodeon viewers voted them the Best Female Actresses of the Year for the film *It Takes Two* in 1996.

•They won this award again in 1998 for their roles as Mary-Kate and Ashley Burke on *Two of a Kind*.

•The girls played themselves in a 1998 episode of the soap opera *All My Children* and appeared as guest stars in an episode of *7th Heaven* in 2000.

•Mary-Kate was honored with a Daytime Emmy nomination in 2002 for her role in *So Little Time*.

•They received the first ever DVD Premiere Franchise Performers Award in 2003 for their phenomenal success in the DVD market.

•Throughout their careers, Mary-Kate and Ashley have been featured in more than 100,000 newspaper stories, they have been on the cover of dozens of magazines around the world, and they have appeared more than one hundred times on TV talk shows and programs like NBC's *Today* and *The Tonight Show with Jay Leno*.

MARY-KATE

FULL NAME: Mary-Kate Olsen (no middle name)
BIRTH DATE: June 13, 1986 (about two minutes
   after Ashley)
HAIR COLOR: Blond
EYE COLOR: Blue-green
FEATURES: Left-handed
                   One inch shorter than Ashley
                   A freckle on her right cheek
                   Rounder face
FAVORITE HOBBIES: Horseback riding, yoga
FAVORITE SHOES: "Sandals, but we call
   them flip-flops."
FAVORITE STORES: Boutiques in Los Angeles and
   New York City and Rome
FAVORITE CLOTHING: Watches, funky necklaces,
   blue jeans, T-shirts, cashmere sweaters
FAVORITE TELEVISION SHOWS: *Will & Grace*,
   Friends
FAVORITE MOVIE: *Best in Show*
FAVORITE KIND OF BOOKS: Real-life books,
   no fantasy
FAVORITE ACTORS: Cameron Diaz and Drew
   Barrymore
CELEBRITY CRUSH: Luke Wilson

FAVORITE SCHOOL SUBJECT: Creative writing
LEAST FAVORITE SCHOOL SUBJECT: Math
PICK A NUMBER: 8
WHAT'S IN HER PURSE: Lip gloss, gum, wallet, cell phone
FAVORITE SPORTS: Basketball and hockey
FAVORITE EXERCISE: Yoga
FAVORITE ANIMAL: Horse
COLLECTS: Candles
SATURDAY NIGHT ROUTINE: Dinner and a movie with friends
RISE AND SHINE: "I like to wake up early!"
DRINK OF CHOICE: Ice-blended mocha
FAVORITE FOOD: Sushi
FAVORITE VEGGIE: Broccoli
FAVORITE ICE CREAM: Mocha
FAVORITE GUM FLAVOR: Strawberry
FAVORITE COLORS: Maroon and blue
HOLIDAY OF CHOICE: Christmas
DESCRIBE YOURSELF: "Outgoing."
IN THE FUTURE: "I see myself going to college, acting in and producing feature films, and continuing to run our company."

ASHLEY

FULL NAME: Ashley Fuller Olsen (Fuller is her
   mom's maiden name)
BIRTH DATE: June 13, 1986 (about two minutes
   before Mary-Kate)
HAIR COLOR: Blond
EYE COLOR: Blue-green
FEATURES: Right-handed
                  An inch taller than Mary-Kate
                  Oval face
FAVORITE HOBBIES: Yoga and golf
FAVORITE SHOES: Flip-flops
FAVORITE STORES: Boutiques in Los Angeles,
   New York City, and Rome
FAVORITE CLOTHING: Accessories, accessories,
   accessories
FAVORITE TELEVISION SHOWS: *Will & Grace*,
   Friends
FAVORITE MOVIE: *Waiting for Guffman*
FAVORITE KIND OF BOOKS: Mysteries and
   historical fiction
FAVORITE ACTORS: Julia Roberts and Drew
   Barrymore
CELEBRITY CRUSH: Ben Affleck
FAVORITE SCHOOL SUBJECT: Math

LEAST FAVORITE SCHOOL SUBJECT: English
AFTER-SCHOOL ACTIVITIES: Yoga, homework, hanging out with friends
PICK A NUMBER: 8
WHAT'S IN HER PURSE: Lip gloss, cell phone, wallet, and day planner
FAVORITE SPORTS: Football and hockey
FAVORITE EXERCISE: Pilates (at the moment)
COLLECTS: Music
SATURDAY NIGHT ROUTINE: Dinner and hanging out with friends
RISE AND SHINE: "I like to sleep in!"
DRINK OF CHOICE: Chai tea latte
FAVORITE FOODS: Angel hair pasta with tomato and basil sauce, sushi
FAVORITE VEGGIE: Broccoli
FAVORITE ICE CREAM: Cookie Dough
FAVORITE COLORS: Yellow, purple, and blue
HOLIDAY OF CHOICE: Christmas
DESCRIBE YOURSELF: "Organized, loyal, and fun."
IN THE FUTURE: "I see myself going to college, acting in and producing feature films, and continuing to run our company."

TWO of a kind™
BOOK SERIES

Based on the hit television series

mary-kate olsen · ashley olsen

TWO of a kind Diaries

Dare To Scare

Mary-Kate and Ashley are off to White Oak Academy, an all-girl boarding school in New Hampshire! With new roommates, fun classes, and a boys' school just down the road, there's excitement around every corner!

Coming soon wherever books are sold!

Don't miss the other books in the TWO of a kind™ book series!

- ❑ It's A Twin Thing
- ❑ How to Flunk Your First Date
- ❑ The Sleepover Secret
- ❑ One Twin Too Many
- ❑ To Snoop or Not to Snoop?
- ❑ My Sister the Supermodel
- ❑ Two's A Crowd
- ❑ Let's Party!
- ❑ Calling All Boys
- ❑ Winner Take All
- ❑ P.S. Wish You Were Here
- ❑ The Cool Club

- ❑ War of the Wardrobes
- ❑ Bye-Bye Boyfriend
- ❑ It's Snow Problem
- ❑ Likes Me, Likes Me Not
- ❑ Shore Thing
- ❑ Two for the Road
- ❑ Surprise, Surprise!
- ❑ Sealed With A Kiss
- ❑ Now You See Him, Now You Don't
- ❑ April Fools' Rules!
- ❑ Island Girls
- ❑ Surf, Sand, and Secrets

- ❑ Closer Than Ever
- ❑ The Perfect Gift
- ❑ The Facts About Flirting
- ❑ The Dream Date Debate
- ❑ Love-Set-Match
- ❑ Making A Splash!

Real **Books** for **Real Girls**™

Watch out for the 2004 calendar!

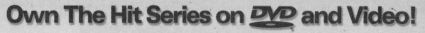